DISCOVER
ROCKS AND MINERALS

Predominant artwork & imagery source:
Shutterstock.com

This edition copyright 2021

North Parade Publishing Ltd.

3–6 Henrietta Mews,

Bath,

BA2 6LR, UK

Printed in China.

Contents

Structure of the Earth

Our solar system came into existence from a cloud of space dust and gas. This was then squeezed into a hot mass called a solar nebula. As this matter became more dense, a hot ball formed in the center and the remaining debris began to revolve around it. Earth formed from the accumulation of some of this material.

Origin of Earth and Other Planets

About 4.6 billion years ago, our solar system was nothing more than a cloud of dust and gas. Due to gravity, these materials collapsed into themselves, forming the Sun in the center and other materials revolving around it. Over time, the dust and gas drew toward each other, forming planets like Earth.

The lighter gases like hydrogen and helium were swept away by the solar winds and they formed the gas giants, Jupiter, Saturn, Neptune, and Uranus. The heavy, rocky materials were left behind and formed the terrestrial planets of Mercury, Venus, Mars, and Earth.

▶ *The early Earth was a hot planet with burning hot rocks and fumes. It was incapable of supporting life.*

Did You Know?

Earth is called a "Goldilocks planet." This means that Earth has everything to support living organisms, such as liquid water, oxygen, carbon dioxide, and resources.

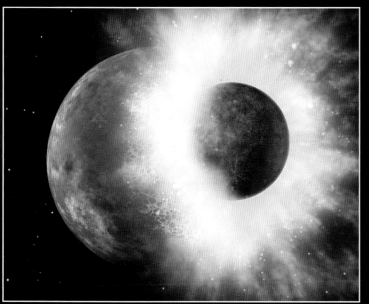

The Moon Is Born

During the time when collisions with asteroids and other such bodies were common, an object about the size of a small planet is thought to have struck Earth and sent a large mass flying into space. This is how Earth's satellite, the Moon, is thought to have formed.

▲ *A collision with a planet-sized body caused the Moon to form from Earth.*

Earth's Core

Earth has a hot and dense core, which is made up mostly of solid, pure iron. This core alone is about the size of the Moon and is 12,600 degrees Fahrenheit! The outer core of the Earth is molten liquid and is made up of iron and nickel. At around the same time that the Earth's core formed, it also developed a magnetic field.

FASCINATING FACT!

The core spins much faster than Earth itself! The inner core and the outer core spin in opposite directions. Every 400 years or so, the core is a full turn ahead of the Earth.

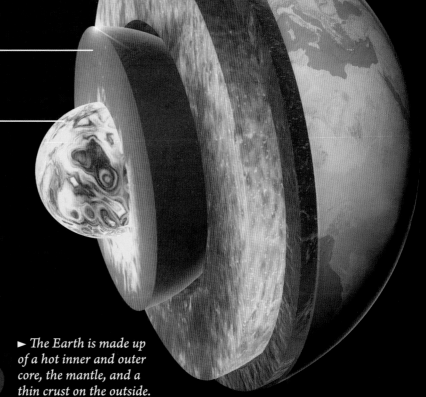

Outer core

Inner core

FASCINATING FACT!

Many precious metals found on Earth are thought to have been brought by asteroids that struck the planet millions of years ago.

► *The Earth is made up of a hot inner and outer core, the mantle, and a thin crust on the outside.*

The Earth's Crust

Our Earth might look like one solid sphere, but it isn't! There are actually many different layers that make up Earth. From the surface to the center, there are the crust, mantle, outer core, and inner core.

The Outermost Layer

We live on continents that exist on the plates of the Earth's crust, which is its outermost layer. The crust extends 10 miles deep and is made up of rocks and organic material.

The distance between the crust and the core is 4,000 miles! The 10-mile crust therefore seems small when viewed in relation to other layers, as it makes up less than 1% of the Earth's overall size. Even with the most sophisticated and advanced drilling machines, the deepest we have been able to drill into the Earth is about 7 miles, and we have only been able to mine up to 2.5 miles. The Earth's crust is made of rocks of different types, many of which were formed around 2–2.5 billion years ago. The continental crust is much older than the oceanic crust materials!

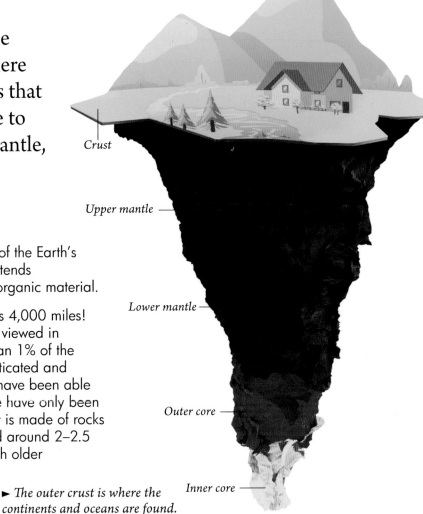

Crust

Upper mantle

Lower mantle

Outer core

Inner core

► *The outer crust is where the continents and oceans are found.*

Plates

You'll be surprised to know that the crust is not simply one solid piece. Instead, it is made up of many pieces, which are called plates. These plates are constantly moving at a very slow rate, so we are generally not aware of it. There are seven major plates and many other minor plates. The major plates are: African plate, Eurasian plate, Antarctic plate, North American plate, South American plate, Pacific plate, and Indo-Australian plate.

► *The plates in the Earth's crust fit into each other like jigsaw puzzle pieces.*

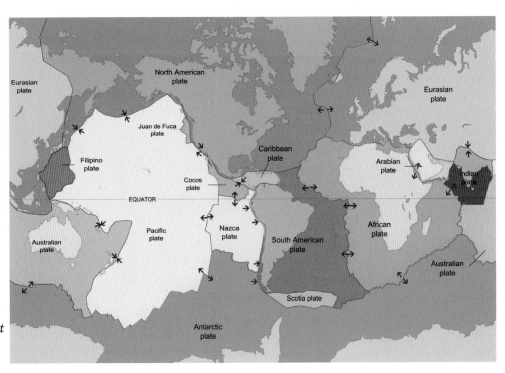

Eurasian plate

North American plate

Eurasian plate

Juan de Fuca plate

Filipino plate

Caribbean plate

Arabian plate

Indian plate

Cocos plate

EQUATOR

Pacific plate

Nazca plate

African plate

Australian plate

South American plate

Australian plate

Scotia plate

Antarctic plate

Continental and Oceanic Crust

Continental crust: The continental crust is covered by land and is mostly made up of granite, sedimentary rocks, and dead animal and plant matter.

Oceanic crust: The oceanic crust is very different from the continental crust in terms of composition. It is mostly made up of basalt from lava flowing out of underwater volcanoes.

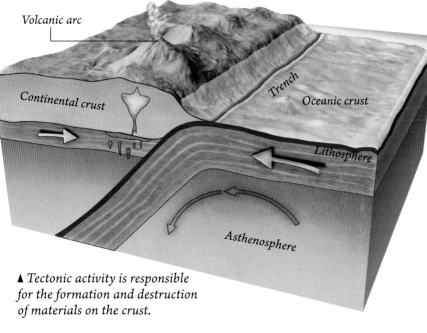

Volcanic arc

Continental crust

Trench

Oceanic crust

Lithosphere

Asthenosphere

▲ *Tectonic activity is responsible for the formation and destruction of materials on the crust.*

Continental Drift

It was Alfred Wegener who first proposed the idea of "continental drift" in 1912. He noticed that the shapes of continents seemed to fit together like jigsaw puzzles, for example South America and Africa. A few other scientists had also noticed this. They observed that the fossils around the shores of different continents were also similar. Since continental plates could move, it was proposed that millions of years ago, all the continents were connected in one super-continent called Pangaea. The continents drifted and moved over centuries to their present locations. In a million years, the Earth will be markedly different from how it is now!

Pangaea

Eurasia

North America

South America

Africa

India

Tethys Ocean

Australia

Antarctica

Laurasia and Gondwana

North America

Eurasia

Africa

South America

India

Tethys Ocean

Australia

Antarctica

Modern world

Arctic

North America

Arctic Ocean

Eurasia

South America

Africa

India

Indian Ocean

Antarctica

▲ *Continental drift causes the continents to move around over time.*

Mountains

Mountains are natural landforms that rise high above the surrounding land and can be seen from miles away. Mountains are much taller and steeper than hills, and are typically at least 2,000 feet in height. When many mountains are found together, they are referred to as mountain ranges. The Himalayas are an example of a mountain range.

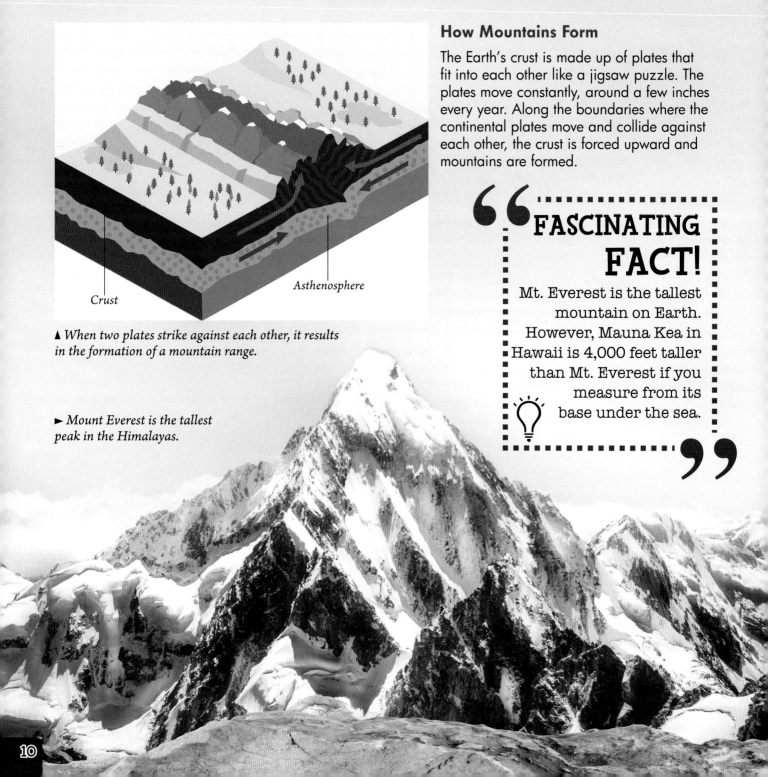

Crust

Asthenosphere

▲ *When two plates strike against each other, it results in the formation of a mountain range.*

► *Mount Everest is the tallest peak in the Himalayas.*

How Mountains Form

The Earth's crust is made up of plates that fit into each other like a jigsaw puzzle. The plates move constantly, around a few inches every year. Along the boundaries where the continental plates move and collide against each other, the crust is forced upward and mountains are formed.

" FASCINATING FACT!

Mt. Everest is the tallest mountain on Earth. However, Mauna Kea in Hawaii is 4,000 feet taller than Mt. Everest if you measure from its base under the sea. "

▲ *The Alps in Switzerland are an example of fold mountains.*

Types of Mountains

Fold mountains are the most common type of mountains found on Earth. The Alps in Europe, the Rocky Mountains in the United States, the Himalayas in Asia, the Andes in South America, and the Urals in Russia are all fold mountains. The folds were formed when the plates collided, their edges crumbled, and the crust was lifted up.

Dome mountains form when magma pushes its way through the crust, but doesn't quite reach the top surface. The rocks then cool and form a mountain. The Black Hills in the United States are an example of a dome mountain range.

▲ *Mauna Kea in Hawaii is a volcanic mountain that is taller than Mt. Everest if measured from its base under the sea.*

Volcanoes can also lead to the formation of mountains. **Volcanic mountains** are the direct result of volcanic activity. They form when magma pushes out from the crater and the material from the eruption collects around it. Mauna Kea, Mauna Loa, and Mount Fiji are volcanic mountains.

▲ *The Black Hills are a range of dome mountains.*

Earthquakes

When the Earth's surface rumbles and shakes, it is called an earthquake. The tremors caused by earthquakes can often be devastating.

How Do Earthquakes Occur?

The Earth's surface is made up of around 20 plates that are constantly moving past each other. They don't move particularly quickly. In fact, geologists have estimated that the fastest moving plate moves only around 6 inches a year. Earthquakes happen when the plates slip past one another. The surface where the plates slip is called a fault. While this is one common reason for an earthquake to occur, it can also be caused by nuclear testing, volcanic activity, and landslides.

Earthquakes happen more often than you think. In fact, millions of earthquakes occur across the Earth every time the plates knock against each other. Most of the time, we don't even know there has been an earthquake because the tremors may be very weak or it may occur under the sea. In fact, the shaking caused by an earthquake is never the reason for danger. It is the destruction of buildings and structures that causes most of the catastrophe.

Powerful earthquakes, on the other hand, can be felt easily. They can damage buildings, other structures, and landscapes. They can also cause landslides, tsunamis, and floods.

Did You Know?

The deadliest earthquake in recorded history occurred in China in the year 1556 and killed nearly 830,000 people.

▶ *An earthquake is dangerous mainly due to the destruction of buildings in heavily populated areas.*

Richter Scale

When an earthquake occurs, it causes vibrations called "seismic waves" that travel through the Earth's surface. These seismic waves are recorded and studied so that we can understand the origin and intensity of earthquakes. The Richter scale is a system that measures these waves and classifies the strength of every earthquake.

If you have ever heard a reporter talking about an earthquake, you would hear how much it measured on the Richter scale. This scale of measurement was devised by Charles Richter in 1935. Although we can measure its strength, there is still no sure way to predict when or where an earthquake will occur.

The Richter scale is recorded using the numbers 1 to 10, with 1 being insignificant and anything above 7 being dangerous and capable of causing much damage.

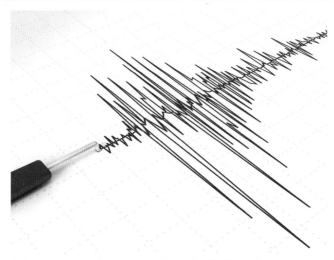

▲ *A graph records seismic activity indicative of an earthquake.*

Ring of Fire

There is a coastal belt of the Pacific Ocean, which is a hot spot of volcanic eruptions, fault lines, and plate movement that is called the "Ring of Fire." Around 80 percent of the world's largest earthquakes occur in this region.

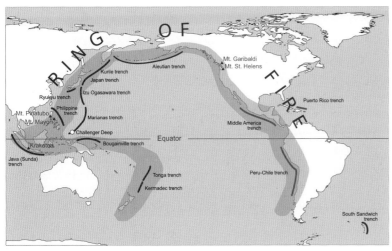

◄ *The "Ring of Fire" is a region of intense volcanic and seismic activity.*

Construction Matters

In Chile, an 8.8 magnitude earthquake killed more than 700 people. In Haiti, a 7.0 magnitude earthquake killed more than 200,000 people. This great difference in death tolls was because of the quality of building materials and construction style. Most buildings in Chile conformed to strict regulations and standards.

If a region is prone to earthquakes, the best way to protect the people living there is to invest in earthquake-resistant buildings. Although no building can be made completely resistant to earthquakes, how well it survives depends on how it is constructed and the kind of technology used.

Earthquake-Resistant Structure

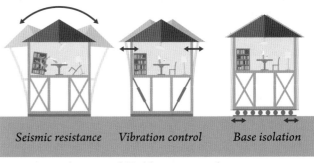

Seismic resistance   *Vibration control*   *Base isolation*

▲ *Engineers design and build structures that can withstand earthquakes.*

Volcanoes

A volcano is an opening in the Earth's crust through which hot magma from deep within the Earth's surface erupts. When the rocks under the Earth's surface become really hot, they melt into a thick liquid. Lava then flows out of the crater in a dramatic eruption, which can sometimes cause widespread damage.

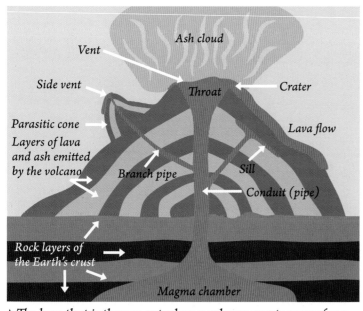

Ash cloud

Vent

Side vent

Throat

Crater

Parasitic cone

Layers of lava and ash emitted by the volcano

Lava flow

Branch pipe

Sill

Conduit (pipe)

Rock layers of the Earth's crust

Magma chamber

▲ *The lava that is thrown out when a volcano erupts comes from a magma chamber deep down.*

> **FASCINATING FACT!**
>
> Lava that erupts underwater is called pillow lava because it spreads and forms pillow shapes.

Active or Dormant?

Volcanoes are classified as being active, dormant, or extinct, based on their activity. An active volcano has either erupted recently or it is assumed that it will erupt in the near future. A dormant volcano has not erupted in a very long time but can potentially erupt at any time. An extinct volcano is not expected to erupt again.

Mount Vesuvius in Italy is considered to be one of the most dangerous and violent volcanoes on Earth! The ancient city of Pompeii was completely buried in lava and volcanic ash after the eruption of Mount Vesuvius in AD 79.

► *Pompeii was an ancient city near Naples that was completely destroyed by a volcanic eruption.*

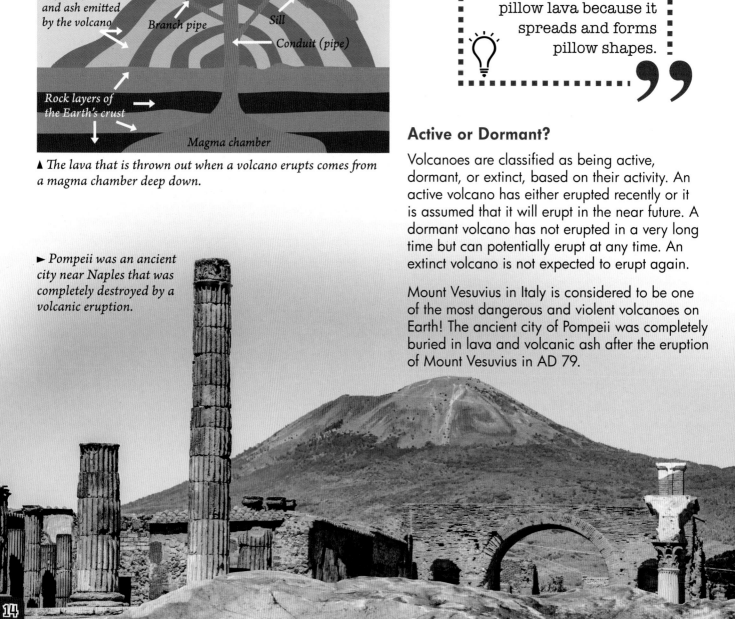

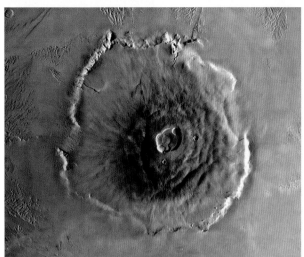

Volcanoes: The Record Holders

The tallest volcano in our solar system is not on Earth, but on Mars and is called Olympus Mons. It is 16 miles tall, which is nearly three times the height of Mt. Everest!

The most volcanic activity in our solar system is on Io, one of Jupiter's moons. So frequent and intense are the volcanic eruptions that Io's surface is constantly changing.

On Earth, the largest volcano is Mauna Loa and the tallest volcano is Mauna Kea—both are located in Hawaii.

◄ *Top view of the tallest volcano in the solar system—Olympus Mons on Mars.*

▲ *Ol Doinyo Lengai is unique for the black-colored and comparatively cooler lava it ejects.*

Types of Volcanoes

Fissure vent: A fissure vent is an opening through which lava erupts without an accompanying explosion. A fissure vent can extend from the volcano's summit to the base.

Stratovolcano: A stratovolcano is made up of many layers of accumulated lava and volcanic ash. This type of volcano has a steep slope and a symmetrical cone structure.

Shield volcano: Shaped like a shield, this volcano is formed of thin layers of lava. Since the lava that flows out tends to be runny, they typically form flat slopes.

Lava dome: This volcano is formed by thick lava that hardens around the vent. Also called a volcanic dome, it can form to a height of several hundred feet.

Fissure vent

Shield volcano

Stratovolcano

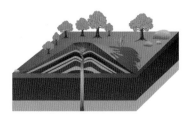

Lava dome

▲ *Volcanoes are classified into different types based on their physical structure and nature.*

Rock Formation

A rock is a solid mixture of mineral crystals that have been fused together naturally over millions of years and make up the crust of the Earth. Rocks are found just about everywhere; some rocks are no bigger than one grain, while others are enormous. A rock formation is a unique and spectacular formation of one or more rocks that have been weathered and eroded.

Rocks, Rocks Everywhere

Different rocks can be found in different regions of the world. The rocks that you see today were formed after thousands or even millions of years. The Earth's crust and the mantle are made up of silicate rock. Together, these two layers are referred to as the lithosphere. It is here that tectonic plates are found and rocks are formed and re-formed continuously in a process known as the rock cycle.

Rock Types

The three common types of rocks are:

Igneous rocks: Formed by cooling liquid magma that has emerged from under the Earth's surface.

Sedimentary rocks: Formed from compacted sediments deposited from eroded rocks.

Metamorphic rocks: Formed by high pressure and temperatures being exerted on igneous and sedimentary rocks.

► Bryce Canyon in Utah has distinct, spire-shaped rock formations.

▲ *Tall and jagged cliffs are found along the coasts of Ireland and many other countries.*

Types of Rock Formations

Rock formations, also referred to as rock structures, are found across the Earth. Geologists have classified them into different types based on certain similarities. Some of the most common ones are:

Cliff: A cliff is usually found near the coast, where mountains meet sea. A cliff is formed over thousands of years through weathering of rocks by water and other forces of nature. Sedimentary rocks readily form cliffs, but igneous rocks like granite or basalt can also sometimes form cliffs.

Peak: Many mountains have a pointed, pyramidal peak on the top. It can also be referred to as a glacial horn. A peak is formed by erosion caused by a divergence of different glaciers from a central point.

▲ *Monument Valley in Colorado is a classic example of a mesa rock formation.*

Mesa: A mesa is a prominent rock formation with an elevated land area and a flat, tablelike shape on the top. It is also called a table hill and usually forms in hot, arid regions. It is formed by the weathering and erosion of weaker layers of rocks above.

Stack: A stack refers to a vertical column of sedimentary or igneous rocks close to the seacoast. They are formed by the constant weathering caused by waves. A stack can also form due to the collapse of a natural arch formation.

Canyon: A canyon is formed by erosion activity over a long time on a plateau. It can be caused either by wind in arid regions or a combination of wind and water near regions close to rivers.

▲ *A mountain's peak is its tallest point, rising up several miles above sea level, and is usually capped with ice.*

Igneous Rocks

All rocks that formed on Earth were initially igneous rocks. Igneous rocks are formed when hot magma slowly cools down and solidifies. The minerals in the magma form bigger and bigger crystals. When enough crystals form and they start to set together, an igneous rock has formed.

How Do Igneous Rocks Form?

Igneous rocks can form deep under the Earth's crust or on the surface. Igneous rocks that form on the surface of the Earth are able to cool down quickly, whereas those under the crust, where temperatures are very high, might take thousands of years to cool down. This is the reason why igneous rocks are classified into two types: intrusive rocks that are produced below the surface and extrusive rocks that are produced on the surface. Extrusive rocks have fine grains, as they cool quickly, whereas intrusive rocks are mostly coarse-grained.

Extrusive igneous rocks cool quickly, and as a result these rocks are fine-grained or have a lack of crystal growth.

Intrusive igneous rocks are formed from magma that cools slowly, and as a result these rocks are coarse-grained.

▲ *Igneous rocks form either outside or inside the surface and are called extrusive or intrusive rocks, respectively.*

Some of the most common igneous rocks include:

Basalt: A dark, fine-grained type of volcanic rock.

Granite: A common rock used in construction. It is made up of 25 percent quartz.

Tuff: A rock formed from volcanic ash.

Obsidian: A type of volcanic glass that forms quickly and has sharp edges.

Gabbro: A dark rock type made up of coarse grains of crystals.

Pumice: An unusual type of lightweight rock with bubbles. Pumice is formed when molten rock is rapidly thrown out of a volcano.

Types of Igneous Rocks

The term "igneous" means "fire." Igneous rocks form from the solidification of hot, molten magma that occurs quickly outside or slowly inside the Earth's surface. Intrusive rocks and extrusive rocks have their own distinctive features. Gabbro and granite are examples of intrusive rocks while basalt, obsidian, and pumice are extrusive rocks. It is unlikely to find organic matter or fossils embedded in igneous rocks, given that they are formed under extreme heat and pressure differences.

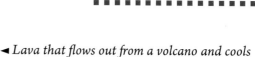

" FASCINATING FACT!

About 95% of the Earth's crust is made up of igneous rocks. "

◄ *Lava that flows out from a volcano and cools rapidly forms extrusive igneous rocks.*

Did You Know?

There are at least 700 different types of igneous rocks!

Giant's Causeway

The Giant's Causeway is thought to have been formed 50 to 60 million years ago. It is a magnificent geological formation of interlocking basalt columns formed by an ancient volcanic eruption. Millions of years ago, the intense volcanic activity resulted in molten basalt flowing through chalk beds. As the lava cooled, it split and formed about 40,000 basalt pillars! These pillars look like smooth stepping stones.

► *The Giant's Causeway is made up of interlocking basalt columns. It is a UNESCO World Heritage Site.*

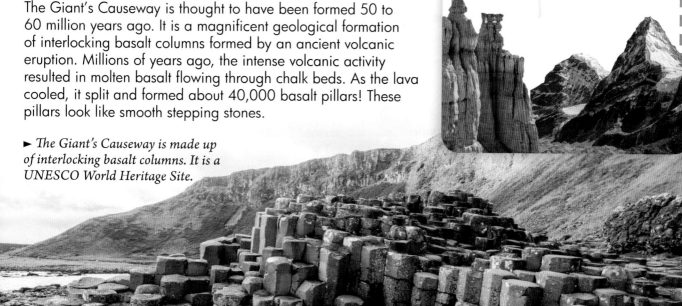

Sedimentary Rocks

Sedimentary rocks are formed from sediments that are deposited along the shores of lakes and oceans over thousands of years. The sediments that make up a sedimentary rock come from sand, mud, and pebbles. These sediments contain minerals and organic matter, all of which gets compressed over a very long time to form solid layers of rock. The layers formed on a sedimentary rock are called strata.

Types of Sedimentary Rocks

There are many types of sedimentary rocks. Some of them are:

Limestone: Made up of deposits of calcium carbonate and may also contain fragments of shells and mud. It is usually formed in lagoons.

Chalk: Made up of soft limestone and the microscopic skeletons of marine plankton.

Flint: A hard, crystalline type of sedimentary rock made of quartz. Flint was used in the Stone Age by early humans to form sharp tools.

▼ *A characteristic feature of sedimentary rocks is the layers, also called "strata."*

FASCINATING FACT!

Limestone caves can be huge and complex. The passages in Mammoth Cave in Kentucky are over 230 miles long!

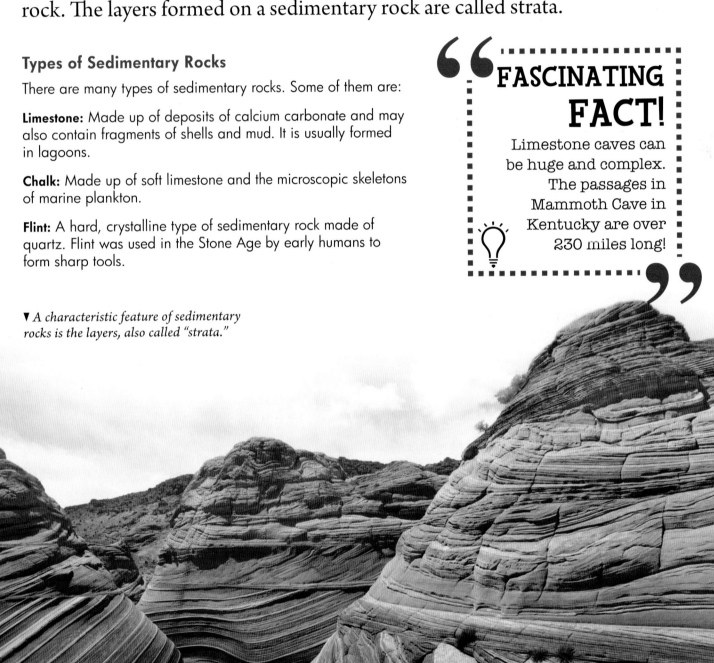

Limestone　　　*Chalk*　　　*Flint*　　　*Sandstone*

Mudstone　　　*Shale*　　　*Conglomerate*

Sandstone: Sand, compressed and cemented together, forms sandstone. This rock is formed from sediments deposited by rivers, the sea, and wind.

Mudstone: Made up of fine grains of clay particles pressed together over thousands of years. This type of sedimentary rock forms in calm waters like lakes, lagoons, and the undisturbed waters of the deep sea.

Shale: Flaky mudstone is called shale.

Conglomerate: This type of rock is made up of pebbles larger than 2 millimeters in size cemented together. They are usually formed by sediments deposited by fast-flowing rivers and beaches.

Did You Know?

Halite is a sedimentary rock and is crushed and purified to produce table salt.

Caves

Limestone caves are interesting geological features. Do you know how these caves are formed? We know that limestone is made up of calcium carbonate and can easily dissolve in acid. Limestone deposits located underground are dissolved by acidic water. This acidic water eats through the limestone deposits, forming hollow caves and underground chambers. In fact, most caves form in regions that have rich limestone deposits.

▶ *Mammoth Cave in Kentucky is a series of limestone caves that stretch across many miles.*

Metamorphic Rock

*M*etamorphosis is a Greek word that means "change in shape." When a caterpillar turns into a butterfly, we call it metamorphosis. It is not just living things that can undergo this process—rocks can too! When igneous and sedimentary rocks are subjected to either very high temperatures or pressures, they turn into metamorphic rocks.

Formation of Metamorphic Rocks

Since temperature and pressure always play a fundamental role in forming metamorphic rocks, we are therefore able to say where they usually form. They form in places where large sections of the Earth's plates are pushing against each other. They also form when hot, liquid magma pushes through other rocks, which heats them up and raises the pressure. Metamorphic rocks have a crystalline structure.

▼ *Marble caves in General Carrera Lake, Chile, have been naturally carved out of solid marble.*

FASCINATING FACT!

Marble has been used for construction and architectural purposes for more than 2,000 years.

Gneiss

Quartzite

Slate

Migmatite

Schist

Marble

Amphibolite

Serpentinite

Types of Metamorphic Rocks

There are different types of metamorphic rocks:

Gneiss: Gneiss rocks are covered in stripes and are made up of grains of minerals.

Quartzite: This rock is made of quartz and is caused by the metamorphism of sandstone.

Slate: Slate is formed by the metamorphism of shale and can easily split into thin pieces.

Migmatite: A banded and granular metamorphic rock with light-colored bands formed by partial melting.

Schist: This particular rock type has a large amount of mica.

Marble: Marble is formed when limestone undergoes metamorphism.

Amphibolite: A dark, heavy rock, made up of coarse grains and with weak foliation.

Serpentinite: It is made up of a mixture of different serpentine minerals and has a variable grain size.

Did You Know?

Metamorphic rocks that form closer to the Earth's surface can split or flake into layers of different thickness. This process is called "foliation."

Taj Mahal: A Marble Monument

The Taj Mahal in India is constructed entirely of marble. It was built in the year 1654 and it is a tomb built by the Mughal emperor Shah Jahan for his third wife, Mumtaz, whom he loved dearly. He wanted the Taj Mahal to be an outstanding masterpiece. Hundreds of elephants were employed to transport the marble and other materials from different locations.

▲ The Taj Mahal is one of the seven wonders of the modern world.

The Rock Cycle

The rocks on Earth don't stay the same forever—they undergo changes all the time. The rock cycle is a continuous process by which igneous rocks change into sedimentary rocks, which in turn change into metamorphic rocks—or back into igneous rocks. This is a long process that occurs over millions of years!

The Ever-Changing Rocks

We do not know where the starting point of the rock cycle is—all we know is that it has been happening for many years.

Sedimentation is the process by which rock particles or layers are formed over thousands of years. When this layer becomes compact and the layers get cemented together, sedimentary rocks are formed.

The sedimentary rocks that are underground become heated and are subject to pressure, and so they slowly transform into metamorphic rocks.

Some metamorphic rocks not only get really heated up, they also melt and turn into a type of liquid rock called magma. This magma comes from deep inside the Earth's region called the mantle. The magma is forcefully ejected out through a volcano. The magma flows out, cools down, and turns into solid rock over time, which produces igneous rocks.

> **FASCINATING FACT!**
>
> In order to transform a metamorphic rock into magma and then into igneous rock, it requires a temperature of at least 2,000 degrees Fahrenheit.

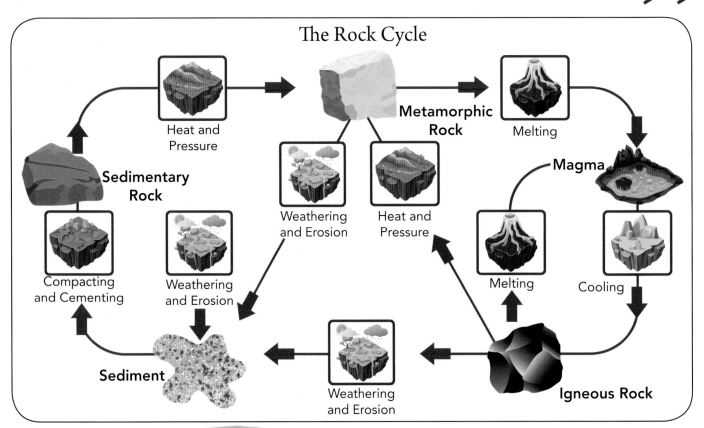

The Rock Cycle

Heat and Pressure

Metamorphic Rock

Melting

Magma

Sedimentary Rock

Weathering and Erosion

Heat and Pressure

Compacting and Cementing

Weathering and Erosion

Melting

Cooling

Sediment

Weathering and Erosion

Igneous Rock

Nature's Influence

Some areas of rocks are pushed slowly upward, as more rocks form underneath. This process is called uplift. Weathering can result in the breakdown of rocks on the Earth's surface; the three major types of weathering are physical, chemical, and biological.

▲ *A rocky area eroded by seawater displays hollowed-out crevices everywhere.*

Different Forces Acting on Rocks

Physical forces, including rainfall and alternating cold and hot temperatures, can also cause rocks to contract and expand and eventually break up.

Different chemical substances, especially pollution, can cause the formation of acid rain, which can also cause rocks to wear away.

Trees are the main biological weathering agents. Who knew the roots of trees could be so powerful that they can make their way through cracks in the rocks and eventually shatter them!

▲ *Cliffs form as wind and water cause erosion along the coasts.*

After the rocks are broken down into smaller fragments, wind and water carry them away in a process called erosion. They are taken to other places and deposited along the shores of lakes and seas. They accumulate and form layers to form sedimentary rocks. This cycle is continuously repeated.

◄ *Trees with sturdy roots can break through layers of rock and erode them gradually.*

What Is a Mineral?

Minerals are naturally occurring substances on Earth. Many minerals are very useful to us and are extracted on a large scale. They have specific physical and chemical properties that are unique to them. While some minerals are made up of a single element, others are made up of a mixture of elements.

Minerals on Earth

So far, at least 5,000 different minerals have been discovered on Earth. Of these, most are very rare. Only about 100 minerals are present in abundance. In fact, only about 15 minerals make up the rocks that are commonly found on Earth.

▼ *A close-up of quartz crystals embedded in rock. Quartz comes in a variety of colors.*

Did You Know?

Some of the most common minerals on Earth are bauxite, cobalt, quartz, talc, feldspar, and pyrite.

1	2	3	4	5
Talc	Gypsum	Calcite	Fluorite	Apatite
6	7	8	9	10
Orthoclase	Quartz	Topaz	Corundum	Diamond

Mohs Scale of Hardness

This is a measure of the scratch resistance of a material. It is named after the scientist Friedrich Mohs, who came up with this scale for measuring hardness of minerals. As the hardest material on Earth, diamond is measured as 10, which is the highest rating on the scale, while soft talc is listed as 1.

Features of minerals

Minerals are classified based on certain properties like:

Color: Minerals can be described by their color. For instance, graphite is black in color and is used in pencil leads.

Hardness: A mineral is classified based on its ability to scratch glass.

Luster: A mineral can be described based on how glossy, dull, metallic, or shiny it looks.

Streak: This refers to the mineral's color in its powdered form.

Antimony ore	Arsenopyrite	Barite ore	Bismuthinite	Bornite	Bauxite	Celestine
Chalcopyrite	Chromite	Native copper	Cuprite	Galena	Dolomite	Ferruginous quartzite
Limonite	Bismuthinite	Magnetite	Magnesite	Molybdenite	Pisolite	Perovskite
Psilomelane	Pyrite	Rainbow pyrite	Scheelite vein	Sphalerite	Titanite	Wolframite

▲ *Minerals vary in colors and textures.*

What Is a Crystal?

A crystal is a special type of solid material that is formed naturally by repeating patterns of molecules. These patterns help to form unique structures and shapes. The word "crystal" is derived from the Greek word *kryos,* which means "ice cold." This is because, in ancient times, people thought that crystals were ice that was so frozen, it would never melt!

Crystallization

The process by which crystals form is called crystallization. The natural process of the formation of a crystal occurs when liquid rock (magma) cools down slowly and gathers into uniform, repeating patterns. A crystal has atoms arranged in a specific, orderly manner, in any one of the seven crystal lattice patterns.

Crystals come in a variety of colors, shapes, and sizes depending on what material they are made of.

Did You Know?

Water that hardens into a single, big snowflake is a type of crystal. But a frozen ice cube isn't because it doesn't have a uniform crystal structure like a snowflake.

▲ *A cluster of purple amethyst crystals embedded in a rock.*

◄ *A snowflake is a transient crystal structure. Every snowflake has a distinct crystalline pattern.*

28

▲ *Gemstones derive more value after they are polished and cut to make them attractive.*

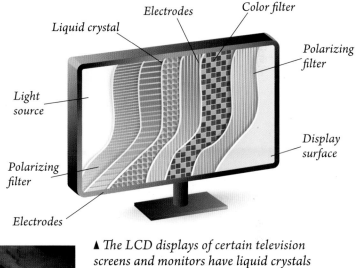
Uses of Crystals

Many crystals are used in jewelry, because of their beautiful colors and patterns. Some of the best-known crystals are gems and precious stones such as emeralds, rubies, and diamonds.

Apart from design and accessories, crystals that are made of minerals are also used for many other purposes. They are used in electronic equipment like transistors and radios, televisions, and LCD/crystal display screens in computers, as crystals allow the image to appear more clearly and vividly.

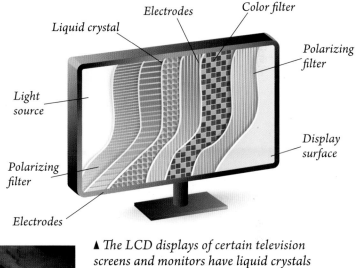

Electrodes
Color filter
Liquid crystal
Polarizing filter
Light source
Display surface
Polarizing filter
Electrodes

▲ *The LCD displays of certain television screens and monitors have liquid crystals for clear and crisp images.*

▲ *The Giant Crystal Cave in Mexico has gigantic gypsum crystals, some of which are 40 feet in length.*

What Is a Gemstone?

Most gemstones are made from large, colorful crystals, and they sparkle and shine in a number of different colors. Gems are mined from the Earth and are then cut and polished by specialists, to be used in jewelry or other decorative objects.

Precious Gems

The rarest gemstones, such as rubies, sapphires, diamonds, and emeralds, are known as precious gems, and are especially beautiful and expensive.

Diamonds are perhaps the most famous and sought-after gems of all. When they are first mined (dug up from the ground), diamonds are rough and dull. Only by cutting and polishing them do they become bright and sparkly like the ones you might have seen in items of jewelry.

> ## FASCINATING FACT!
>
> There are more than 4,500 known minerals in the world, but only around 100 are used as gemstones!

► *The larger, clearer, and more sparkly a diamond is, the more valuable it becomes.*

Did You Know?

Diamond is the hardest natural material on Earth, which means that only a diamond can cut a diamond!

Semiprecious Gems

While precious gems are very rare and are found only in certain parts of the world, other stones, such as quartz and garnet, are mined worldwide. These more common stones are often referred to as semiprecious stones. Even though they are more readily available, only a tiny proportion of these stones may be of gem quality, so they are still desirable and often very beautiful.

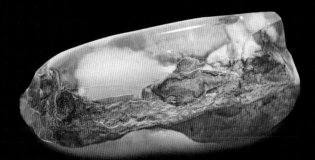

▲ *Amber is formed from a fossilized substance called resin, which comes from trees!*

Birthstones

People in ancient times believed that gems came from the heavens, and that certain stones were lucky for those born in particular months of the year. Can you find your lucky stone in the list below?

January	May	September
Garnet	**Emerald**	**Sapphire**
February	June	October
Amethyst	**Pearl**	**Opal**
March	July	November
Aquamarine	**Ruby**	**Topaz**
April	August	December
Diamond	**Peridot**	**Turquoise**

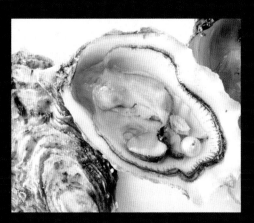

Organic Gems

Most gems come from rocks, but some, such as pearl, amber, and coral, come from organic things. Pearls, for example, are formed when a tiny piece of food or sand becomes trapped in an oyster's shell. The oyster covers it with a mixture of minerals and proteins, which eventually makes a pearl!

Gem Cutting

Gemstones are usually cut and polished to enhance their beauty and color. The process of cutting and polishing gems is called lapidary. There are a few basic methods of lapidary used to transform a rough gem into a polished and attractive piece of art. The final product is used for making jewelry or artifacts.

Tumbling

Rough gemstones are tumbled (or turned at low speeds) in a rotating barrel with abrasives and water for many days, or even weeks! Abrasives are materials that are hard and rub against the gemstones to smoothen their surfaces. Hard minerals or synthetic stones are used as abrasives. Tumbling and then washing carefully, and then repeating these steps, gradually produces smooth stones of attractive shapes.

◄ Tumbled gems from the rotating tumbler are collected for further processing.

▼ *A specially designed device is used for cutting diamond.*

▲ *Turquoise, before and after processing. Polished and shaped turquoise looks elegant and beautiful.*

Carving

This is the most challenging and artistic of all the techniques. Any design that is cut on top is called "intaglio," or relief carving. Carving is done simply for artistic beauty.

▲ *A device used in the past for faceting gemstones.*

Faceting

If you look closely at a diamond, you will notice that the surface has many geometrically arranged, flat surfaces. Each flat surface is called a "facet." Faceting is an important step for bringing out the brilliance of certain gems, as the light that enters the gemstone is reflected off the facets to produce a sparkling effect. A faceting machine is used to make precise cuts.

▶ *Gems are cut into specific shapes, and depend on color and nature to bring out their maximum beauty.*

Cabbing

Also called "cabochon cutting," cabbing is another common technique used in gem cutting. As with tumbling, there is a cabbing machine that does the job, and this process is slightly more complicated than tumbling.

Did You Know?

Lapidary has been practiced for a very long time! Cylinders made of the gem serpentine were common in 3000 BC.

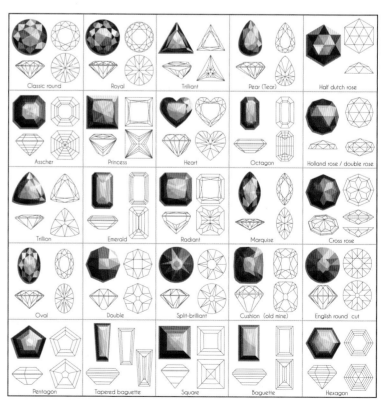

Classic round | Royal | Trilliant | Pear (Tear) | Half dutch rose
Asscher | Princess | Heart | Octagon | Holland rose / double rose
Trillion | Emerald | Radiant | Marquise | Cross rose
Oval | Double | Split-brilliant | Cushion (old mine) | English round cut
Pentagon | Tapered baguette | Square | Baguette | Hexagon

Metals from Rocks

Metals can sometimes be stored inside rocks in the form of minerals. Such a rock that holds a metal is called an ore. Ores take millions of years to form and are finite. Miners explore deposits on all continents as well as the ocean floors to extract metals to meet our continuous demands.

How Are Metal Ores Formed?

Metal ores accumulate in different ways. Some metals are brought to Earth by meteorite impacts. Volcanic eruptions can also bring out metals to the surface from deep underneath the Earth's layers. Seawater can also circulate through cracks in the Earth's crust and deposit minerals around hydrothermal vents.

▼ *A foundry worker is controlling the smelting of iron in a furnace.*

Did You Know?

Gold is a nonreactive metal that doesn't fade or tarnish even after remaining buried for millions of years! We have mined about 80 percent of all the gold present on Earth.

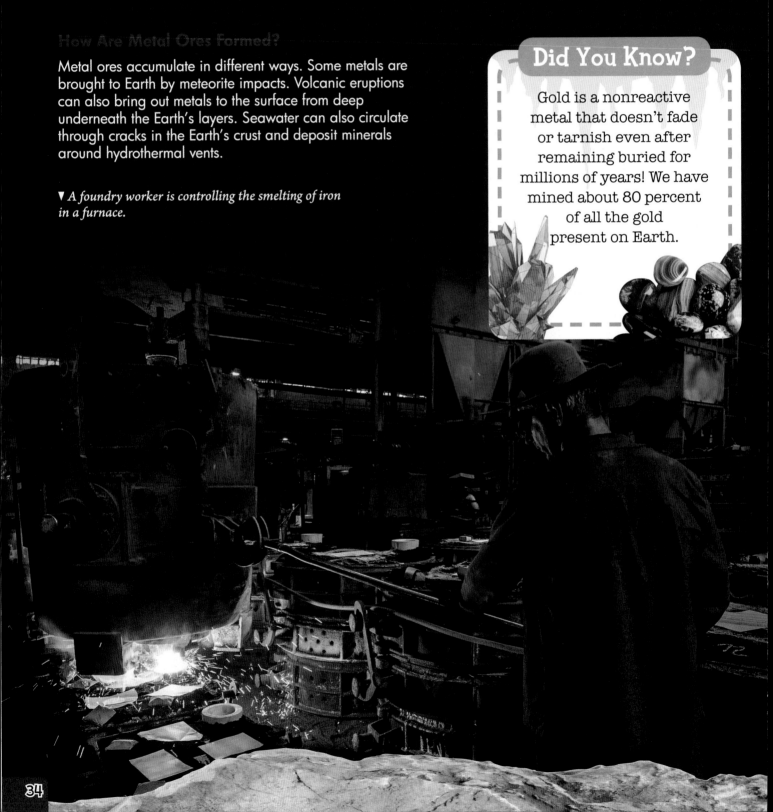

▲ *Mined gold nuggets are melted and shaped into bars or ornaments.*

Extracting Metals

Certain chemical processes can be used to separate the metal from the rock. Sometimes, we're lucky enough to find a useful metal in its pure form. You can sometimes find gold and silver nuggets in rocks, simply by breaking the rock apart.

However, metals like aluminum, copper, and iron can often occur in combination with other elements. For instance, copper occurs in combination with other elements, such as copper carbonate in malachite ore. To extract only the copper out of the ore, the malachite has to be heated and then treated with chemicals to obtain pure copper. There are many chemical reactions involved in taking the metals from the rocky ores.

Some common techniques are:

- Electrolysis
- Bioleaching
- Smelting
- Chemical reaction

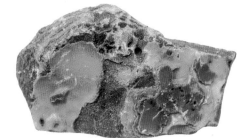

▲ *Top: Green malachite (copper ore)*
Bottom: Galenite (lead-silver ore)

Purification of Metals

After extraction, metals need to be purified for them to serve different purposes. This is achieved through different methods. The type of method used depends on the metal and its chemical nature. Some common techniques include electrolysis, distillation, and liquation. Distillation is ideal for volatile or unstable metals like zinc or mercury; electrolysis is used for purifying different metal types such as copper, lead, and nickel; liquation works best for metals with a low melting point.

▶ *Electrolysis is the chemical basis for large-scale purification of certain metals.*

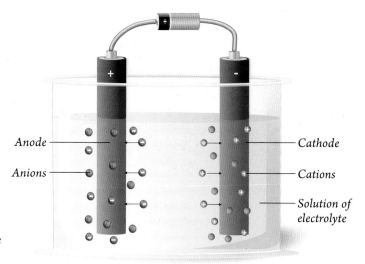

Anode

Anions

Cathode

Cations

Solution of electrolyte

Mining

Most metals and minerals are buried deep inside the Earth's crust. Mining is the process by which these minerals and metals are extracted from the ground. Some examples of what is extracted through mining include iron, manganese, copper, tin, nickel, tantalum, cassiterite, bauxite (an ore of aluminum), gold, silver, diamonds, and a variety of precious and semiprecious stones.

Types of Mining

There are many different types of mining, depending on what material is being extracted. Some common types of mining techniques include:

Gold panning

Since gold is heavier than water, sand thought to contain gold particles is rinsed in water and collected.

Open pit mining

These are simple open pits with terraced side walls. Some minerals and uranium are extracted by digging such pits.

▼ *The Bingham Canyon Mine in Utah is the deepest open pit ever dug.*

▲ *Gold panning is a simple method of using plates on shallow waters to collect silt and sift it for gold nuggets.*

◄ *The interior of a shaft mine can be dangerous, as it is hot and lacks oxygen, making it difficult for workers.*

Shaft mining

A vertical pit is dug until a "seam" is reached. A seam is a region that is rich in minerals. At that point, the pit is dug horizontally, in order to mine all the minerals along the seam. Shaft mines are dangerous, as there is the risk of suffocation and extreme heat within the mine.

▲ *Lignite extracted from a strip mine in Germany is used for electricity production.*

Strip mining

A seam of mineral ore is sometimes extracted by removing the top layers of soil and rock on top of it. The machines used for this, such as a drag line and bucket wheel excavators, are some of the largest construction vehicles ever built.

Quarrying

Mountains with useful material such as granite are usually quarried for the breaking apart of large rocks. Earlier, dynamite had been used to crack apart the hard rocks before the workers worked on them with hammers and wedges. Today, powerful mechanized saws do the work instead!

▲ *A quarry is where huge quantities of rocks are broken apart and transported.*

Fossils

We would have never known about dinosaurs were it not for fossils! Fossils are preserved remains of plants and animals. Usually, plants, animals, and organic matter undergo decay and are destroyed completely, unless they are preserved in a special way.

Studying Fossils

Fossils are most often found embedded in rocks, but they can also be found in sand or gravel. Many of the fossils that have been discovered had remained buried for millions of years. Studying fossils helps scientists learn about the different animals that lived on Earth millions of years ago, and understand the process of evolution.

▼ *Paleontologists work patiently for hours to dig around fossils and extract them carefully.*

How Fossils Form

When a dead animal sinks into mud, it doesn't decay due to the fact that it has no exposure to air. The remains of the animal thus stay undisturbed for millions of years. The minerals present in the mud coat the dead animal and turn it into stone.

There are many different ways by which fossils can form:

Amber: The complete bodies of insects have been preserved in a type of hardened tree sap called amber and preserved intact.

Carbonization: A process where all components of an animal are dissolved except for the carbon, which leaves a residue in the shape and outline of the animal.

Mold: A mold or a cast is an impression left behind by an animal. The animal leaves behind a hollow mold that fills up with minerals to create an exact replica.

▲ *A frozen mammoth fossil preserved in ice is extracted.*

Freeze preservation: Ice is excellent for preserving animals intact for thousands of years as long as the ice doesn't melt! The woolly mammoths were preserved intact in the glaciers of the Arctic.

Mummification: A dry climate and the absence of moisture is the perfect recipe for fossil formation. Instead of decay, the organism dries out completely and its remains are preserved.

▲ *Fossilized dinosaur eggs coated with mineral deposits have been recovered.*

Permineralization: Mineral deposits form a detailed cast of the organism. Carbonate, silicate, and pyrite can form fossils.

▲ *An insect preserved intact in a piece of amber.*

▲ *A fish that has been carbonized and embedded in rock.*

▲ *The molds and casts of ammonites, which are ancient marine organisms.*

> ## FASCINATING FACT!
> Fossils have been found in all parts of the world. Most preserved fossils have been found in sedimentary rocks such as limestone, shale, and sandstone.

The Fossil Record

All the fossils we have dug up so far—and others that remain under the Earth, waiting to be discovered—are collectively referred to as the fossil record. The fossil record refers to the placement of fossils across the different layers of the Earth.

Lessons in Fossils

Some of the simplest organisms have been found in the oldest rocks and deepest layers that people have dug into. Fossils of more complex organisms have generally been found in newer rocks. The fossil record is evidence that shows how complex organisms have evolved from simple organisms.

Imagine four billion years of evolution and natural selection being unrolled in front of your eyes! A fossil record is just like a movie, except that only a few frames of the movie are preserved, and many are yet to be dug up. All of the fossils that are available tell us a story about a constantly changing planet.

Since only the fossils of animals with hard shells or bones remain, we have virtually no clues or evidence about soft-bodied organisms. The fossil record goes back to trace the different organisms that lived and survived, and shows how similar or different they are from present-day plants and animals. In fact, the fossil record is the major evidence for evolution.

It reveals many diverse organisms that lived in the ancient oceans that we call the Cambrian Sea. We have found ancient organisms that are similar to modern animals, as well as organisms that are unrelated and very different from the creatures we are familiar with today.

> ## FASCINATING FACT!
> Studying fossils of preserved flowers has shown us that flowering plants evolved from nonflowering plants.

▼ *Fossilized remains of a dinosaur provide information about its body and habits.*

▲ Clear imprints of an ancient trilobite reveal much about its structure.

▲ The fossils of flowers and other plant parts have also been preserved intact over millions of years.

Exciting discoveries

Thanks to fossils, we now know about many creatures that lived millions of years ago, such as dinosaurs and woolly mammoths. Paleontologists have also unearthed fossils and molds of many marine plants and animals that resemble lichens, algae, seaweed, jellyfish, soft corals, annelid worms, and sea anemones.

▲ We know about the existence of large woolly mammoths with giant tusks because of the fossils that were discovered.

Horse Fossils and Evolution

While we do not have complete fossil records for most organisms, we do have a fossil record of horses. We know that horses were once as small as dogs and lived in rain forests 60 million years ago. It is this fossil evidence that shows us just how different horses were a million years ago. By looking at these differences, we can understand how the horse has evolved over time, to adapt to its changing environment. An example of this adaptation is the developing of suitable hooves for living on plains and grassland.

Did You Know?

The oldest known fossils are those of organisms resembling cyanobacteria that lived in the oceans near Australia about 3.5 billion years ago.

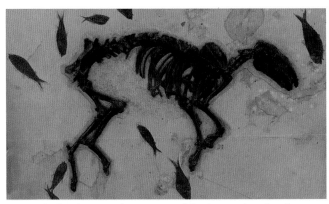
▲ Fossil of a dog-sized ancestor of the horse that lived millions of years ago.

Rocks from Space

Nearly 100,000 tons of material from outer space falls onto the Earth's surface every year! While most of it is in the form of cosmic dust or small fragments, some objects can be very heavy and large in size. The rocks that fall onto the Earth are called meteorites.

Meteorites

Meteorites are rocky fragments that have been separated away from asteroids found between Mars and Jupiter. Space rocks can also arrive from the Moon, comets, and Mars. They orbit the Sun and are occasionally pulled out of their orbit by the Earth's gravitational pull. People who have reported seeing meteorites falling have described them as glowing fireballs, accompanied by a sonic boom.

Apart from the fact that they are valuable curiosities from outer space, meteorites are also useful for studying the origin and age of our solar system.

▼ A crater is a large, hollow space created by the impact of a sizable meteorite strike on the Earth's surface.

Did You Know?

The Vredefort crater in South Africa is the biggest impact crater on Earth, estimated to be 185 miles in diameter when it originally formed about 2 billion years ago!

Iron

Stony iron

Stone

Chondrite

Carbonaceous chondrite

Martian

Types of Meteorites

Iron: Made up of iron as the major component; also includes nickel, and comes from the core of large asteroids.

Stony iron: A mixture of stony material and iron.

Stone: Once a part of the outer crust of an asteroid or a planet. A freshly fallen stone meteorite will have a black fusion crust.

Chondrite: One of the most common types of meteorites to arrive on Earth. It is similar in composition to the planet's crust and mantle.

Carbonaceous chondrite: Similar in composition to the Sun, but contains less volatile components.

Achondrite: Closely identical to basalt found on Earth, and believed to have originated from another planet or asteroid.

Lunar and Martian meteorites: These are much rarer than other types of meteorites. When meteorites strike on the surface of the Moon or Mars, they fire fragments into space that sometimes get pulled to Earth.

> **FASCINATING FACT!**
>
> The Nantan meteorite that fell in China in 1516 had a combined weight of over 20,000 pounds. This is one of the few meteorite specimens on display that you can actually touch if you wish!

Lunar Rocks

Between the years 1969 and 1972, plenty of rock samples from the Moon (about 842 pounds) were brought back to Earth to study. This includes rocks, pebbles, sand, and dust from the surface of the Moon. By studying them, we have learned that the Moon could have formed from the debris of a planet-sized body striking Earth about 4.4 billion years ago.

► *This lunar rock is one among the different rock samples collected from the Moon by astronauts.*

Minerals around the World

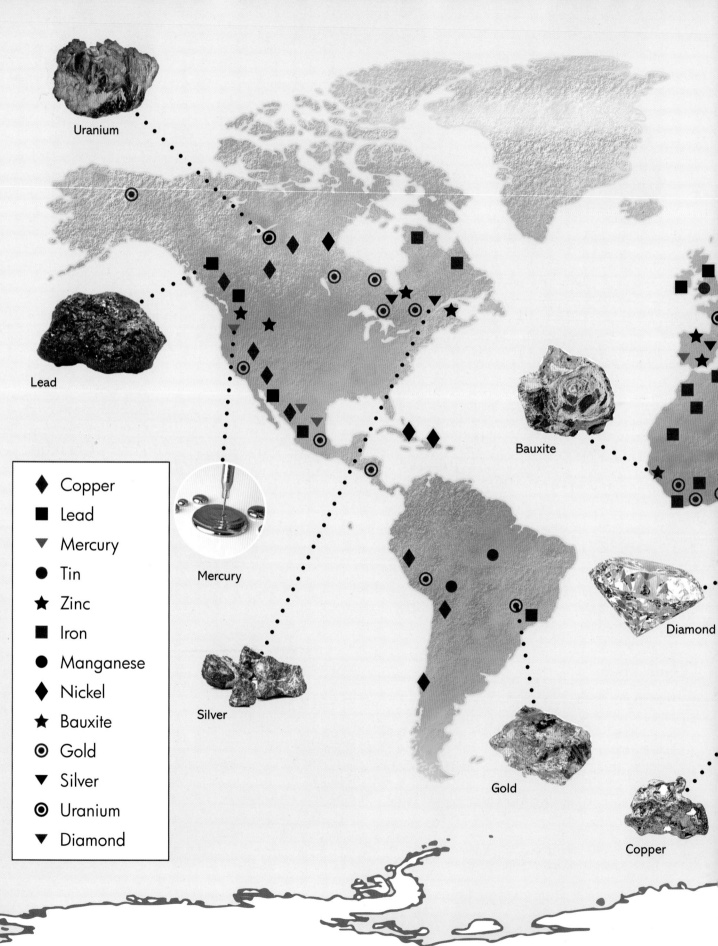

Uranium

Lead

Mercury

Bauxite

Diamond

Silver

Gold

Copper

Legend:
- ◆ Copper
- ■ Lead
- ▼ Mercury
- ● Tin
- ★ Zinc
- ■ Iron
- ● Manganese
- ◆ Nickel
- ★ Bauxite
- ◉ Gold
- ▼ Silver
- ◉ Uranium
- ▼ Diamond

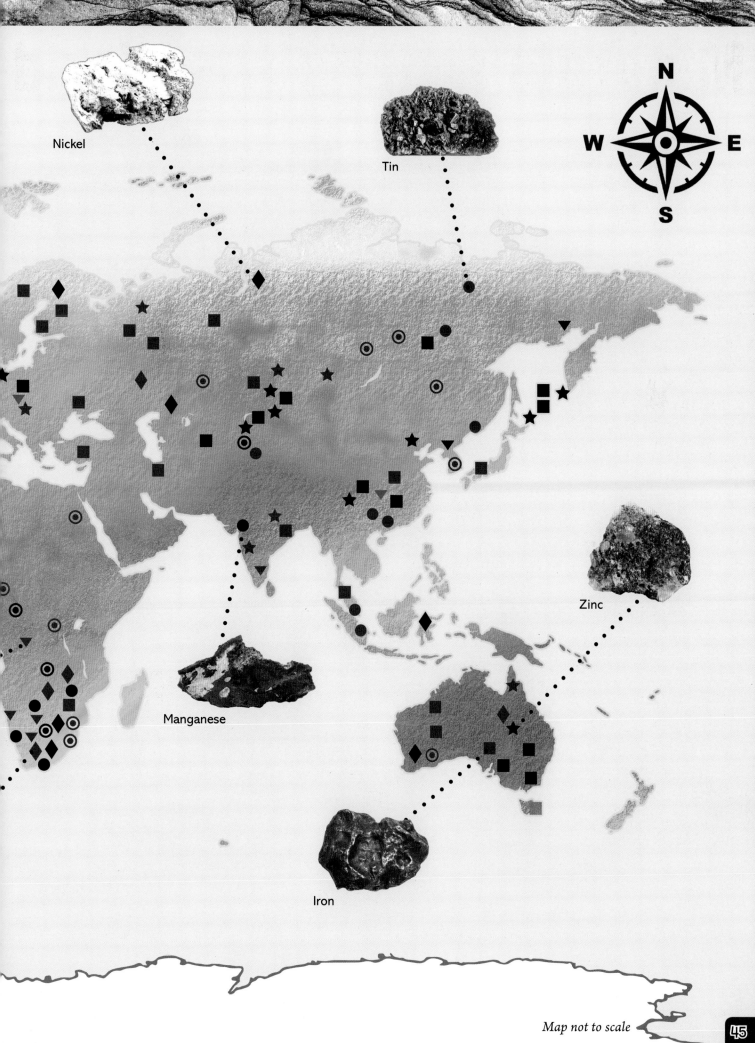

Nickel

Tin

Zinc

Manganese

Iron

Map not to scale